Carn of Bars at Pool (near the Hell Bay Hotel).

INTRODUCTION: BRYHER, SAMSON AND THE NORRARD ROCKS

The islands that sit right on the western edge of Scilly – Bryher, Samson and St Agnes – are the most typically 'off-island' in their character: a wonderful combination of wild heath-clad hills, upstanding carns and curved sandy bays. Their character is formed by the perpetual conflict between sea and land here and, even on the sunniest of summer days, you can sense how unnervingly wild it can be in bad weather. During storms, waves crash right over Shipman Head on the northern tip of Bryher, sending cascades of spray into New Grimsby Sound. At times like that, Hell Bay is an accurate description.

The Norrard Rocks give the southern end of Bryher some protection from the roughest seas. The wind is less easily pacified, and the houses at Pool and Great Par huddle for protection behind any slight rise in the ground. This area around Popplestones, Great Par and Rushy Bay is the most beautiful coastal scenery in Scilly. The main settlements at the Town and Norrard sensibly retreat behind the shelter of Watch Hill.

Grey seal in a garden of seaweeds.

All the Scillonian off-islands have experienced periods where they've been abandoned completely by humans, sometimes several times over since prehistory. Samson is the most recent example; it was last abandoned in the mid 19th century. The roofless and ruined houses lend it a wistful air, a reminder of how precarious living on this beautiful western margin can be. It's a hugely attractive isle and it remains so vividly locked in your memory that even many years later, when you recollect a visit, you're drawn back with a startling intensity to the carns, the tombs and the sea.

The Norrard or Northern Rocks sit a little higher in the water than the Western Rocks, but they are still too inhospitable to support much life beyond the transitory visits of breeding sea birds. Seals bask on the boulder beaches and pup here in the autumn, but life has only a shaky hold on these exposed rocks. However, when you look over the side of a boat you get a rather different impression. The Garden of the Maiden Bower may sound like an English cottage garden full of roses and apple blossom, but really it's a garden of seaweeds – of tangle, furbellows, cuvie and the hypnotic waving fronds of dabberlocks. If you're lucky, you'll glimpse a shadow slipping between the watery sunbeams, because the only maidens that live here are mermaids and seals.

Looking over Great Par to Gweal Hill and Gweal Island.

BRYHER

The root of the name Bryher is in the Cornish word *brea* meaning *hill*, and the island is a chain of hills all linked by low-lying necks and sandy bars. It would only need sea levels to rise by a few metres for the southern part of Bryher to transform itself into a group of five or six separate islands. All these hills – Gweal, Timmy's, Watch, Heathy and Samson – are too exposed and windswept to be cultivated, and Bryher's ninety residents make their lives in a relatively narrow zone, compressed between hill and shore. A few fields and houses inch up the hillsides at the Town and Norrard, but even here the hills dominate, giving Bryher a rough-hewn character closer to Samson and Gugh than to the other inhabited islands. Bryher's west coast is particularly lovely. Here are all the ingredients that make Scilly such a profoundly beautiful place: curved bays filled with granite boulders; sandy beaches backed by dunes with every inlet guarded by a carn-topped hill.

Ferries and sightseeing boats land at Church Quay when the tide permits, switching to Anneka's Quay on

The Bar (Anneka's Quay), looking over to New Grimsby on Tresco.

the Bar at low water. A popular itinerary for visitors from other islands is to catch a morning ferry to Bryher, spend the morning exploring, then hop on a lunchtime ferry to Tresco. After lunch at the New Inn or one of the other island cafes, it's an easy walk to the Abbey Garden. Ideally, you'll be able to pick up a return ferry from the southern tip of Tresco at Carn Near Quay.

In this book we'll head clockwise around Bryher, first following the east coast south to Samson Hill and Rushy Bay, then heading up the west coast to Great Par and Shipman Head Down. The whole island is a circular walk of about 6.6km (just over 4 miles).

THE SOUTHERN PART OF BRYHER

The easiest way to get your bearings on Bryher is to stroll along the island's main road which links Bryher's three tiny settlements – Norrard, the Town and Pool – doing a loop around Timmy's Hill on the way. Although it won't take you to the most rugged parts of the island, you will be able to enjoy a selection of cafés, galleries and shops on the way to Great Par.

We'll start by following the coast south from the quays to Samson Hill and then up the west coast to Pool and the Hell Bay Hotel, returning on the island road, a circular walk of 3.2km (2 miles) from Church Quay.

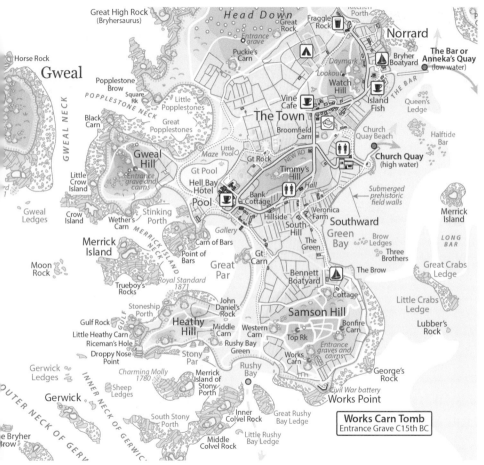

For a longer walk continue past Pool to Popplestones where you can turn inland under Puckie's Carn following the edge of the fields to Norrard, a 4.5km (2¾ mile) circular walk.

If your ferry lands at Anneka's Quay it will be low water and you'll probably be able to walk along the sand to Church Quay Beach. Otherwise, follow the island road to the Town. Go straight over the crossroads by the fire station and, after a hundred metres, the road splits either side of the island hall; keep left to Veronica Farm and the coast at Green Bay.

If you land at Church Quay don't follow the concrete track as it turns sharply right (as it heads to the loos and church); instead keep straight ahead at the top of the quay onto a sandy lane. Within a few strides you'll be standing overlooking the beach at Green Bay with Samson Hill standing in the middle distance.

The *Firethorn* crosses Green Bay after landing at Church Quay. Tresco is in the background and Round Island Lighthouse is just visible.

Green Bay and Southward

A line of large stones march across the sand and into the sea at Green Bay, the remains of a 3,000-year-old prehistoric field wall. Presumably more walls like this lie between here and Tresco as both islands are joined at low water by sand flats. On the lowest tides of the year, in the weeks around the spring and autumn equinox (in March and September), you can walk and wade all the way from Green Bay to Crabs Ledge, Plumb Rocks and on to Tresco. These very low tides are something of an event on Scilly, and lots of people take the chance to cross between the islands (you can walk from Samson too). A makeshift drinks bar and food stall is set up on the sand flats midway between the islands (see Tresco Island website for details). If you decide to cross ask for advice from locals and let them know what you're doing and when you're doing it. Ensure you know the tide times and don't set off more than half an hour after low water or in poor visibility. Unfortunately, in the main summer months the tides aren't low enough to be able to cross on foot.

From Green Bay you can either skirt the base of Samson Hill following the coast path to Works Point (an old Civil War gun platform) and Rushy Bay, or take the path inland by the boatyard gate up to Samson Hill.

Standing on Samson Hill and looking over Rushy Bay to the Norrard Rocks.

Rock piles at Stony Par. Castle Bryher stands in the background.

Samson Hill and Rushy Bay

There are panoramic views from the top of Samson Hill over the calm waters east to Tresco (and Round Island Lighthouse), south over Rushy Bay to Samson, and west to the Norrard Rocks. A fine entrance grave sits on a granite outcrop at Works Carn just south and below the main summit, but it can be a little difficult to get to in late summer when bracken and brambles choke the path. The main path descends the western flank of Samson Hill towards Rushy Bay, one of the most popular beaches on Scilly. It gets its name from the marram grass that grows on the dunes here.

Heathy Hill, Stony Par and Stoneship Porth

In late summer this little hill is a good place to watch the sun set behind the Norrard Rocks. On the south side of the hill at Stony Par you'll find a cove full of granite rock piles. On the north side of the hill lies Stoneship Porth, said to be named from the wreck of the *Charming Molly* lost here in 1780. She was on her way to Dublin with a cargo of Portland stone, some of which were salvaged and are said to have been used on the island. Droppy Nose Point is named after a rock shaped like an elephant's head and trunk (there's a similar rock at Dropnose Point on Gugh).

Great Par and Pool

The sight of the beach at Great Par curving into the mid-distance is one of the best views on Scilly, artistically arranged with Great Carn in the mid-distance and the high ground of Shipman Head Down as the backdrop. In the 18th and 19th centuries, Bryher, like all the islands, supplied pilots for ships arriving in the Western Approaches and heading up to Bristol or the channel ports. When the sails of an incoming ship were sighted, a lookout on Timmy's Hill would sound the alert and the gigs would be launched from Pool and race out to meet it. The first boat to get to the ship got the job, so competition was fierce even for those gigs from the

Great Par looking to Carn of Bars with Gweal Hill behind.

same island or crewed by different members of the same family. Pool was home to the famous Bryher gigs *Albion*, *Golden Eagle* and *Czar*.

Mostly it was speed, stamina and seamanship that won the race and the contract, but trickery sometimes played a part too. A lookout might sight a ship but keep it to himself. Then nonchalantly stroll down to the beach pretending to have seen nothing only to give a discreet nod and wink to his crew, who would be in the water and away before the other boats could launch. Bryher had two very fast gigs both built by the Peters family of St Mawes – the *Golden Eagle* built in 1870

and the *Czar* built in 1879. The *Czar* was so fast she was nicknamed 'the cut-throat gig'.

Bryher's closeness to the Norrard Rocks meant that her gigs were often first to reach ships in trouble, and they, as we'll see, helped with rescues of the *Minnehaha* and the *Delaware*. On the day *Czar* arrived on Scilly from St Mawes she helped in the rescue of the *Maipu*, wrecked in Hell Bay, and the *River Lune*, lost south of Annet. Most gig sheds are now derelict or lost under the dunes, but the one that housed the *Golden Eagle* is now the studio of Bryher artist Richard Pearce. Time for food and refreshments at the Hell Bay Hotel.

Gweal Hill and Gweal Island

Gweal comes from the Cornish word element *guel* meaning *grassy* or *enclosed field*. Given the channel that now separates it from Bryher, it's difficult to imagine grazing animals on Gweal today. However, Gweal Neck is very shallow and, as Cornish names often originate at least 500 years ago, it may well have been joined to Bryher at the time. A Bronze Age (2300–700BC) entrance grave and two cairns stand on the summit.

Popplestones

This unusual name seems to come from an English or Yorkshire dialect word *popel* for *pebble*, possibly brought to Scilly after the English Civil War (1642–1651) when the islands received settlers from the north of England, mainly soldiers and their families from the Parliamentarian Army. This was a strategy to dilute the natural Royalist sympathies that had seen the islands hold out for the King even after he fled to exile in France.

The coast path at Little Popplestones now heads uphill to Shipman Head Down. To return to the quays, either take the road across the island from in front of the Hell Bay Hotel or, follow a longer route at the base of the high ground below Puckie's Carn and Great Rock, following the edge of the fields past Bryher Campsite and Fraggle Rock Bar to Norrard.

The *Golden Eagle* gig shed at Great Par and the Hell Bay Hotel.

THE WILD NORTH OF BRYHER

The northern third of Bryher is, just like Tresco, a substantial plateau of exposed and dramatic high ground. It only has a very thin, skeletal soil and everywhere the granite bedrock breaks through so that only the hardiest plants like heather, gorse and English stonecrop survive here. They have to hug the ground to keep out of the salt winds that sweep across the island, and few plants are more than ten centimetres high.

If you land at the Bar the easiest way to Shipman Head Down is to turn right (north) on the main concrete track to Norrard. At the T-junction just before the Fraggle

Rock Bar, the main track curves away right to Kitchen Porth; ignore that, and instead take the track on your left (towards the campsite). After just thirty metres it splits; keep right and follow the hedge and path through a couple of fields as it heads uphill and onto Shipman Head Down.

If you land at Church Quay follow the main track past the church to the crossroads by the fire station. Here you have two options, either turn right for the island shop and on to the Fraggle

Rock Bar (as above), or go straight over the crossroads to the coast at Pool and make your way around the back of Popplestones and up to Shipman Head Down that way.

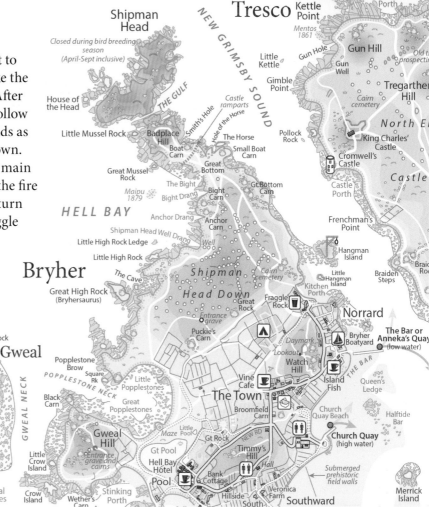

Kitchen Porth looking over to Cromwell's Castle and Castle Down on Tresco.

Kitchen Porth and Hangman Island

Kitchen Porth is a lovely spot for children to play while you sit down outside the Fraggle Rock Bar for lunch and a few drinks. Hangman Island is said to have been where Admiral Blake (see our Tresco book) executed two local guides who deliberately misdirected his forces during the English Civil War (1642–1651). They were supposed to land near Old Grimsby on Tresco but were deceived into landing on the tiny isle of Northwethel instead.

Shipman Head Down

Too exposed to be useful to the living, Shipman Head Down is instead inhabited by the prehistoric dead. The place is one huge prehistoric cemetery, and more than a hundred cairns sit on the surface (not to be confused with *carns*, which are natural rock features). These low, man-made mounds of stone and turf have been greatly eroded over the last 3,000 years and can be difficult to spot, but the longer you look, the more they stand out. Imagine them as low round or oval platforms perhaps half a metre to a metre in height and two to three metres across (although a few examples are twice the size).

Many incorporate natural rock features into their structure and they are almost always sited on rough ground above and away from cultivated areas. In Scilly if you're on top of a hill you're probably standing on one whether you know it or not. Many have a circular retaining kerb of upright stones that make them a lot easier to spot against the general clutter of natural rock. Some, especially on the eastern side of the down, are aligned on, or linked by, tumbled prehistoric walls.

The exact role of cairns is surprisingly unclear. A few are certainly part of prehistoric burial or cremation rituals and have a central stone-lined box, a cist, to hold artefacts or remains (there are good examples on Samson). Sometimes the remains are in the form of ashes from a cremation held in a pottery urn; sometimes an individual appears to have been laid on their side in a foetal position and the cist covered with a slab. Many others appear to have never held artefacts or organic remains.

Unfortunately, the soil conditions on Scilly mean that little organic matter from that time is preserved, and many cairns have been damaged after being dug out by treasure hunters. Here, they obviously form part of a wider ritual landscape, a prehistoric cemetery in use for far longer than the graveyard of today's parish church. A hundred metres north-north-east of Puckie's Carn there is a much larger (but ruined) tomb – possibly an entrance grave – twenty metres wide with a kerb and stone-lined central chamber or passage.

A tumbled prehistoric wall on Shipman Head Down.

Hell Bay and Shipman Head Cliff Castle

It's one of the best places to be after a gale has blown through, when the skies have cleared but a strong sea is still running. The waves that arrive in Hell Bay have often travelled for hundreds of miles so that when they are suddenly slowed by the rough seabed here, they build to a great height to hit the coast with a shuddering thud. Hell Bay then becomes a furious, confused cauldron of foam. Spray caught by the wind lashes the tip of the island, drifting in a cloud across New Grimsby Sound – definitely not a time to be standing on the aptly named Badplace Hill.

The northern tip of Shipman Head Down was fortified in prehistory by an earth and stone rampart, now reduced to just a low bank. Like the Giant's Castle on St Mary's (and possibly Burnt Hill on St Martin's too), it probably dates from around the 1st and 2nd centuries AD when waves of raiders started to harass and harry the West Country. However, the site is so inhospitable (lacking even a water supply) it can never have been more that a refuge of last resort.

Now return across Shipman Head Down for refreshments at one of Bryher's cafes or head to a quay to pick up your boat.

The northern tip of Bryher, looking over Hell Bay to Boat Carn, Badplace Hill and Shipman Head.

The South Hill of Samson. The line of the old deer park wall is visible as are the shadowy outlines of prehistoric fields under the bracken.

SAMSON

Samson is the only uninhabited island on Scilly where sightseeing ferries regularly land, and a visit here is often twinned with a visit to nearby Bryher or Tresco. The island has an almost magical pull on visitors and is often the most vividly remembered part of any holiday on Scilly. Ferries land on the beach at the north end of the island and most people make their way up to the summits of North Hill and South Hill where the prehistoric tombs are sited, although a lower path also meanders along the coast to East Par. The western slopes of North Hill and the southern slopes of South Hill are closed from the beginning of April to the end of September to protect breeding birds (mostly terns and black-backed gulls). There are no shops, cafes or loos on Samson so remember to bring water, sun cream and a picnic with you.

Samson is the classic type of Scillonian isle, a figure-of-eight formed of twin hills connected by a narrow, low-lying neck. It's so neatly proportioned it looks as if someone has designed it or drawn it on a map to bring it into being – an impression confirmed by that other typically Scillonian trait of naming the most beautiful and picturesque places with the most humdrum and prosaic names. Here we have North and South Hill, East and West Par (Porth), a description so terse and pithy it's almost comical when you see the beauty of the place.

The ruins of an early prehistoric settlement lie beneath the sands of East Par. Neolithic (4000–2300BC) flints found here date the site to the centuries around 3000BC. So this may have been one of the pioneer camps on Scilly (like Old Quay on St Martin's) used by itinerant Neolithic hunters and then, when agriculture reached the islands, by settlers and farmers. At that time Samson, along with Bryher, were just the western hills of a much larger single island connected by sand dunes and salt flats to Tresco and to St Mary's where Crow Bar is today. Subsequent sea level rise has flooded these low-lying areas between the islands.

Puffin Island

Great Rag Ledge

Channel Ledge

Bollard Point

John & Mary 1873

Landing Beach

Bar Point

Western slopes of North Hill closed during bird breeding season (April-Sept)

North or Bryher Hill

Black Ledge

Advena 1854

Flea Rock

Long Ledge

Entrance graves and cairns

Samson

SAMSON FLATS

North Hill Tombs
Entrance Graves C15th BC

White Island
Closed during bird breeding season (April-Sept inclusive)

West Porth Ledge

West Par

Submerged prehistoric field walls

White Island Ledge

Neck of Samson

East Par

Green Island

WHITE ISLAND NECK

West Carn of South Hill

Well

Old deer park wall

Closed dur breeding (April-Sept i

Abandoned houses

South Hill

Shag Point

Entrance graves

Tarbarrel Rock
From the wreck of the Otto

Southern tip of Samson closed during bird breeding season (April-Sept inclusive)

South Hill Tombs
Entrance Graves C15th BC

Southward Well Point

Great Minalto Ledges

HMS Colossus

Landing Beach on Samson.

The main Bronze Age (2300–700BC) settlement appears to have been on the southern slopes of South Hill where small hut circles are dotted among the field walls (they are usually lost under the bracken in the summer). The outlines of the small fields are just discernible as shadowy undulations in the canopy of bracken (see the photo on page 16). Both hills are crowned by fine entrance graves, and this, along with Samson Hill on Bryher, Kittern Hill on Gugh, Cruther's Hill on St Martin's and Arthur in the Eastern Isles, were undoubtedly important places where ritual was celebrated and where the dead were interred in these communal tombs. It seems reasonable to assume that each of these places was associated with a specific family or clan that lived close by.

Cultivation at that time appears to have continued between today's islands, and prehistoric field walls are easily picked out from the top of Samson as dark lines beneath the sea. Sea level rise since prehistory has submerged them and, as the tide falls, the dark lines are revealed as seaweed-covered boulders that can be followed across Samson Flats towards Black Ledge. On the lowest tides of the year, it's perfectly possible to walk across to Tresco. The walls were used in the 19th century to catch fish trapped on the falling tide.

The name Samson comes from St Sampson, a 6th century Welsh saint. He's known to have travelled the sea between Wales, Cornwall and Brittany and is venerated at Golant near Fowey and on Guernsey. If he did stop here (we've no direct evidence he did), he can't have stayed for long because he is most well known for founding the monastery at Dol de Bretagne in Brittany, where he died sometime around AD560. About thirty years ago a stone-lined grave was uncovered on the foreshore of East Par, possibly associated with the lost chapel of St Sampson. Subsequent excavations uncovered a timber structure from the 6th century AD and further north the foundations of a later, rectangular stone building, two graves and a rough stone font. So this was probably, like Teän, St Helens and Tresco, one of Scilly's holy islands where a Celtic Christian hermit lived.

After a long period of being uninhabited, Samson seems to have been resettled after the end of the English Civil War (1642–1651) by people from the mainland. We know from census records that by the beginning of the 19th century about forty people were living here in about nine households, mostly members of the Webber and Woodcock families (the Woodcocks are still a well-known family on Scilly). They seem to have reused the 3,000-year-old prehistoric fields on the southern slopes

Entrance grave on South Hill, Samson.

of South Hill. The walls of an old gig shed are sometimes uncovered in the dunes and turf at the north end of West Par, and they must have fished, snared seabirds and collected eggs as well as cultivated the fields. It's probably a mistake to see this simply as a grinding existence; it was little different to the way many communities in West Cornwall lived and the sea was a bountiful, if sometimes capricious, resource to have on your doorstep.

Even in poverty the beauty of the place must have instilled a great sense of belonging. Tamarisk, elder trees and pretty primroses planted by past inhabitants still grow by the abandoned houses and hint at the joy of domestic gardens. In the end though the island was really too small and its resources were too poor to comfortably support a community of forty. Water was difficult to collect and in extended dry periods often had to be brought over in barrels from Bryher. There was no wood for fuel, so the islanders had to rely on burning bracken and collecting what little driftwood washed ashore. In good times there could be few more beautiful places to live, but when poor weather, drought or disease struck it must have felt like a very precarious existence.

The island was hit by a series of droughts in the early part of the 19th century, and by the time Augustus Smith took on the lease of the islands from the Godolphin

Abandoned house on Samson.

family in 1834, most of the inhabitants were destitute. The large waste tips of limpet shells that can still be seen outside the front doors of some of the cottages suggest a population struggling to get by as it takes a great many limpets to feed a family. Augustus Smith provided alternative housing for them on St Mary's, and by 1855 the island was deserted. The last person to leave was Ann Webber, who is said to have laid a curse on Augustus Smith as she left her island home for the final time.

Since then no one has lived here. Augustus Smith built a large wall to create a deer park, but the deer would leave the island at low tide and the project was soon dropped. Part of Samson's attraction comes from the romantic allure of an island abandoned, with its roofless cottages, disused wells and tumbled field walls. The picturesque decay of the abandoned cottages was an inspiration for the poet Tennyson and for Sir Walter Besant, who set the novel *Armorel of Lyonesse* here. For the Victorians, Samson soon became a popular excursion and place to picnic, full of tragic beauty. We still feel that today. More recently, Michael Morpurgo's book *Why the Whales Came* is set here and on Bryher.

The loss of *HMS Colossus*

The *Colossus* spent the summer of 1798 hunting Napoleon's fleet in the Mediterranean, taking part in the Battle of Cape St Vincent and the Battle of the Nile in which Lord Nelson inflicted decisive defeats on the French Navy. She was badly damaged in the encounters and retired to Naples for repairs and celebrations; both were short lived. Napoleon's army was approaching and Sir William Hamilton, the British representative to the Court of Naples and husband of the famous Lady Emma, was forced to evacuate to Palermo but not before his wife's heart missed a beat on meeting Nelson for the first time, the start of a long, passionate affair between them.

Although the *Colossus* was in poor shape, she was forced to make her way under escort to Scilly where she

The carved sternboard from *HMS Colossus* on the seabed.

anchored in St Mary's Sound in late November 1798. A week of southerly gales keep her in Scilly and her already strained and damaged fabric deteriorated further so that on 10th December, when her main anchor cable parted and she was driven onto Southward Well reef, she broke apart in minutes. The crew were saved by local boats, but the ship was a complete loss along with much of Sir William's priceless second collection of Etruscan and Greek pottery (his first makes up the core of the British Museum's collection). The site of the wreck was relocated in 1970, and fragments of shattered vases were recovered from the seabed and the long task of piecing them back together started in the British Museum workshops.

This reconstructed krater (a vessel used to mix water and wine) dates from 440–430BC and shows the return of the god Hephaestus to Olympus. Hephaestus was Hera's son and the god of artisans and craftsman. He made many of the best accessories for the Olympian gods like Aphrodite's girdle and Hermes' winged helmet and sandals. However, Hera took against him and cast him out of Olympus because he was lame. He took revenge on her by constructing a magical gold throne which, once she sat on it, would not let her stand up again. The other gods pleaded with him to release her, but he stubbornly refused and only relented after Dionysus got him drunk and coaxed him back to Olympus. The krater shows Hephaestus on a donkey leading the procession back to Olympus. A satyr follows him playing the pipes and a drunk Dionysus is supported by another satyr. A female satyress brings up the

A Greek krater pieced together from fragments recovered from the seabed around the wreck of *HMS Colossus*.

rear. Some parts of the ship were recovered at the time, and cannons recovered from the wreck now stand as bollards on Hugh Town Quay.

In 2002 a piece of beautifully carved sternboard from the *Colossus* was unexpectedly revealed on the seabed. It was in an incredibly good state of preservation and had obviously been protected by a deep covering of sand since the wreck went down in 1798. A shift in sea currents or conditions must have exposed it, and without its protective covering it had started to deteriorate. It was recovered in 2011, preserved and can now be seen at Valhalla on Tresco. Time Team did a TV show in 2002 – *The Wreck of the Colossus* – and there is lots more information and photos on the *Colossus* (and on the loss of the British Fleet on the Western Rocks in 1707) on the Cornwall and Isles of Scilly Maritime Archaeology Society (CISMAS) website.

Looking over to the Norrard Rocks from Bryher. The taller rock is Castle Bryher with Illiswilgig and Seal Rock behind.

THE NORRARD OR NORTHERN ROCKS

The Norrard Rocks are too small and exposed to ever have been inhabited by humans but the flat rocks around Seal Rock and Scilly Rock, and the sheltered boulder beaches on the Brow of Mincarlo and Illiswilgig, are favoured basking and breeding sites for seals.

Castle Bryher and the Maiden Bower at about twenty-one metres high stand above most of the group. Along with Illiswilgig and Mincarlo, these higher rocks are home to breeding pairs of storm petrels, guillemots, razorbills, puffins, cormorants and gulls. Their rock faces are stained white with streaks of fishy guano, wafts of which catch in the nostrils as you pass by on sightseeing boats. Few plants can endure the exposed conditions on these rocks, and only the hardiest seaside specialists like sea beet and the shingle-loving orache are found here. In some years they are joined by trailing mats of Hottentot fig and Sally-my-handsome, presumably transported here from the gardens of Bryher by nest-building birds.

Sightseeing boats cruise around the rocks and reefs to view the wildlife but don't land here.

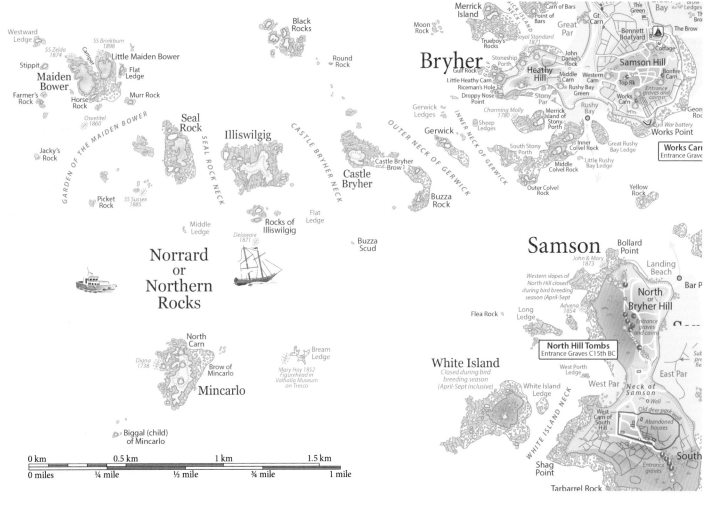

The *Delaware* founders on the Norrard Rocks

In a long history of courageous rescues on Scilly, the rescue of two crew members from the steamship *Delaware* was one of the greatest. On 20th December 1871 the *Delaware* was en route from Liverpool to Calcutta with a crew of forty-four and a cargo of cotton when it was caught in a severe north-westerly storm. At about 3am the Bishop Rock Lighthouse was sighted to the south. By noon the storm had increased to hurricane force and heavy seas were rolling right over her decks. A lifeboat was ripped off its davit, smashing into the roof of the engine room, and she had great difficulty in making any headway at all. The engines were under so much strain that the bearings started to glow red hot and the captain reluctantly ordered them shut down. The *Delaware*, now helpless before the storm, was driven relentlessly towards to the Norrard Rocks.

The crew held their nerve despite the circumstances and rigged up a sail in the hope of steering the ship into the channel between Mincarlo and Illiswilgig. However, it was blown away within seconds of being raised. At that moment the cargo shifted as a set of huge waves swamped the ship, carrying away all the rigging, the remaining lifeboats, the bridge and the captain with it. The ship rapidly took on water and sank.

All this was watched with horror by the inhabitants of Bryher from Samson Hill. Just when hope for survivors was fading, five men were spotted clinging to wreckage and being driven towards White Island. The pilots immediately launched the gig *Albion* in an attempt to rescue the survivors. Four of the seven crew were from the same family. With a gale raging around them, the gig was carried from Great Par to Rushy Bay where it could be launched into a more sheltered sea.

The gig was launched with some difficulty into the sea at Rushy Bay, and the crew had to pull hard to get to the landing beach on the northern tip of Samson. One of the crew, Richard Ellis, was sent up to the top of North Hill to keep a lookout for survivors in the sea and to signal back to Bryher if another boat was needed. Now the gig was launched again and rowed to the Neck of Samson where it was manhandled overland to West Par, the crew struggling to stop it being blown away as they carried it on their shoulders. Finally, already exhausted from their exertions, they launched the gig at West Par.

Large breaking waves pushed the gig almost vertical and progress towards White Island was painfully slow, with two of the crew having to bail continuously just to keep the gig afloat. When they reached White Island one of the crew was put ashore to search for survivors.

The gig *Czar* returns from the stranded *Minnehaha* with cattle lashed to her side.

He found two men, naked and badly injured on the west shore, but to his great surprise, as soon as they saw him they started shouting and throwing stones. It appears that the captain of the *Delaware* used to entertain himself and his crew by recounting stories of murderous Westcountry wreckers, and the two survivors feared they would be killed so that locals could claim salvage on the cargo. After some plain speaking on both sides, the misunderstanding was cleared up and the survivors were rowed back to Samson where everyone collapsed in exhaustion on the beach. The gig *March* was called over to help pull the *Albion* back to Bryher.

Scilly Rock and the wreck of the SS *Minnehaha*

The *Minnehaha* grounded on the Eastward Ledge near Scilly Rock on 18th April 1910 after becoming lost in thick fog on her way from New York to Tilbury. The sea was calm, so the sixty-four passengers on-board were ferried to Bryher without incident. In an attempt to lighten the ship and float her off the rocks before she became a total wreck, the captain ordered all the cargo in the forward holds to be jettisoned. Dozens of live cattle were hoisted into the sea, roped to the sides of gigs and escorted to the safety of Samson. Crates of cigarettes, early American roadsters, sewing machines, carpets

The *Minnehaha* aground on Scilly Rock.

and grand pianos drifted gently away from the stranded ship. One roadster floated all the way to the Wolf Rock, about thirty-three kilometres west of Scilly, where it was recovered by a trawler. Other items were salvaged and towed ashore by islanders who are said to have smoked themselves silly for the next year.

The *Minnehaha* had grounded at low speed, and although stuck fast on the rocks, was not severely damaged. A few weeks later she was pulled free on a spring tide. She continued in service until she was torpedoed by a U-boat near Fastnet Rock in September 1917 with the loss of all hands.

Gig racing on Scilly

Pilot gigs like the *Albion* and *Czar* that took part in the rescues of the *Delaware* and *Minnehaha* are of a type of six-oared boat favoured in Scilly and Cornwall in the 18th and 19th centuries. Their design was robust enough for the open sea but sleek enough to speed out to inbound ships who needed pilots to navigate them up to Bristol or the Channel ports. Gigs from each island on Scilly would compete to be the first to reach an inbound vessel and secure the pilotage contract. St Agnes was well placed to pick up trade from ships arriving from the west, and St Martin's had an advantage for those ships arriving from the north, but every island had its own boats and a lookout on its highest hill.

Throughout the second half of the 18th century and most of the 19th century, pilotage was an important source of island income and gigs would often be owned by extended family groups. There were four pilots based just on St Agnes, supporting the livelihoods of dozens of people. This ready pool of experienced and fit oarsmen frequently risked their lives in rescues using their gigs and later in the 19th century as crew on official lifeboats stationed on St Agnes and St Mary's. Even then the lighter more agile gigs were sometimes preferred to the heavier lifeboats as they were able to swiftly dart in and pluck survivors to safety from rocks and wreckage. A lighter boat also reduced the physical burden on the crew, as a rescue like the *Delaware* could take many hours to complete and crew exhaustion was often a crucial factor in its success or failure.

A few pilot gigs worked into the 20th century but they were finally eclipsed by steam boats in the 1920s and 1930s. The gigs were abandoned and fell into disrepair along with their gig sheds, which can sometimes be made out at the top of even remote Scillonian beaches like Peraskin on St Agnes and at West Par on Samson. They were once thatched with reeds or roofed with red Bridgewater clay tiles, but today they are roofless, their long parallel walls often filled to the eaves with drifting sand. At Great Par on Bryher, painter Richard Pearce has restored the gig shed that once housed the *Golden Eagle* as his studio and gallery.

In the 1970s there was a revival in interest and some of the old gigs were coaxed back to seaworthiness. Today gig racing is a popular sport and there are weekly races in the season – men race on Friday evenings and women race on Wednesday evenings. Courses vary, but the two main ones are a long course from Old Wreck Buoy near Annet to St Mary's Harbour and a shorter, more sheltered course from Nut Rock near Samson. The competitive spirit that existed between the old gigs is alive and well, and races are followed by a fleet of sightseeing boats. The evening usually ends up in a pub.

For a week at the beginning of May each year, crews from Cornwall and as far away as America come to compete for the World Championships on Scilly. A few gigs survive from the 1830s, the heyday of gig design, and are still active. The Bryher gig *Bonnet*, which was launched in 1830, still races, as does the *Czar*, which is today based on Tresco. The St Agnes gig *Slippen*, which took part in the *Thomas W Lawson* rescue, doesn't race now but is occasionally seen out on the water.

Gig races take place every week in the season. The gigs *Bonnet* and *Czar* were both constructed in the 19th century and are probably older than the combined ages of their crews. They took part in the rescues of the *Minnehaha* on Scilly Rock and *Thomas W Lawson* on Annet.

BRYHER ISLAND INFORMATION

INFORMATION

Isles of Scilly Tourist Information Centre
Located above Porthcressa Beach on St Mary's.
www.visitislesofscilly.com
E: info@visitislesofscilly.com T: (01720) 620600

FERRIES AND QUAYS
Church Quay is used at high water and
Anneka's Quay on the Bar, at low water. During
the season, ferries land on the uninhabited
island of Samson (take water, food and sun
cream). Sightseeing boat trips circle the Norrard
Rocks but don't land.

Tresco Boat Services
Daily services run to St Mary's and Bryher plus
a rotating mix of sightseeing, wildlife and trips
to other islands throughout the week. A weekly
plan of services is available at:
www.tresco.co.uk/boats
T: (01720) 423373 E: trescoboats@tresco.co.uk
 @TrescoBoatServices. @TrescoBoats

Bryher Marine Engineering, Steve Hulands
For all your inboard and outboard repair and
servicing needs.
T: 07786235107 E: info@bryhermarine.co.uk

BEST BEACHES
The sheltered beach beside Church Quay
is popular with families. Rushy Bay on the
southern tip of the island is one of Scilly's best
and good for swimming. The long sandy beach
at Great Par catches the afternoon and evening
sun – a good place for a picnic.

CAMPSITE

Bryher Campsite, Norrard
Stunning ocean views, spacious fields and a
friendly, relaxed atmosphere. Bring your own
tent or enjoy a fully-equipped rental Bell Tent.
www.bryhercampsite.co.uk
   @bryhercampsite

SHOPS

Bryher Shop, The Town
www.bryhershop.co.uk
T: (01720) 423601

Bryher Gallery, The Town
Shows work from local makers including
artwork and textiles. www.bryherartist.com
T: (01720) 423665

Golden Eagle Studio, Great Par
Bryher painter Richard Pearce has restored the
gig shed that once housed the *Golden Eagle* as
his studio and gallery. www.bryherartist.com
T: (01720) 423665

ACTIVITIES

Bennett Boatyard, The Green

Isles of Scilly Boat Hire, Bar

Island Wildlife Tours
Naturalist Will Wagstaff leads half and full
day walks around the islands. Programme is
advertised on a noticeboard at Hugh Town
Quay and at the Tourist Information Centre.
www.islandwildlifetours.co.uk
T: (01720) 422212 E: will@islandwildlifetours.co.uk

PLACES TO EAT
Check online or ring ahead as you may need to
book in the summer months and in the quieter
months some cafés don't open every day.

Fraggle Rock Bar & Cafe, Norrard
Open all day in the season, check their
Facebook page for updates.
www.bryher.co
E: fragglerock@bryher.co
 @fragglebryher @fraggle_bryher

Hell Bay Hotel, Great Par/Pool
The highest-rated hotel and restaurant on Scilly.
Overlooks Bryher's rugged west coast. Open
during the day for tea, coffee and lunch in the
bar and terrace plus spa treatments too.
www.hellbay.co.uk
T: (01720) 422947 E: contactus@hellbay.co.uk
   @HellBayHotel

Island Fish, the Bar
Locally caught shellfish and fish to eat in
the cafe or takeaway. Open 1st April to 31st
October, Monday to Saturday, 9.30am to
5.30pm. www.islandfish.co.uk
E: contactus@islandfish.co.uk
 @IOSFish Island Fish Ltd

Olivia's Kitchen, the Town
Take a break from exploring and pop into
Olivia's Kitchen At The Vine. Relax and enjoy
some wonderful food and drink while taking in
the views. Open 7 days a week 9am to 4.30pm.
E: oliviaskitchenbryher@gmail.com
  @OliviasKitchenBryher

GETTING TO SCILLY

The Isles of Scilly are located 40km (25 miles) west of Land's End in Cornwall.

ARRIVING BY CAR

Head for Exeter then follow the A30 to Penzance. The A30 can be very busy on summer Saturdays and bank holiday weekends. To avoid the queues, aim to arrive on the Cornish border (about 1¼ hours from Penzance) before mid-morning or leave it until late afternoon/early evening. Flying from Exeter avoids Cornwall's congested trains and roads in the summer.

Parking in Penzance

You can't take your car to Scilly but there is secure parking at Land's End Airport, Penzance Heliport and in various locations around Penzance. Some secure parking sites are on the outskirts of Penzance so book parking when you buy your travel tickets and make sure you arrange a shuttle bus or taxi to take you to your departure point.

ARRIVING BY TRAIN

Penzance Station is served by direct trains from London Paddington and the North. The Night Riviera sleeper train leaves Paddington late evening and will get you to Penzance by about 8am the following morning. A shuttle bus runs between the station and Land's End Airport (12km/7½ miles) and Penzance Heliport. You will need to book a seat in advance and should aim to leave Penzance Station one hour before your scheduled take-off time. You can also get a taxi from the station forecourt. Passengers for the *Scillonian* can simply walk along the harbour to the Lighthouse Quay.

BY SEA ON THE SCILLONIAN

The *Scillonian III* sails to Scilly from around mid-March to the end of October. It usually departs Penzance at 9.15am with the return sailing leaving St Mary's at 4.30pm but departure times can vary depending on the tide and weather. The journey takes about 2¾ hours and you get a scenic view of the West Penwith coastline on the way.

In the busiest periods, there are two sailings a day, one departing Penzance at about 6am and one at 1pm. The return sailings from Scilly are at 9.30am and 4.30pm. Day trips to St Mary's from the mainland are possible if you leave on the early sailing. Many people book a late flight back on the Skybus to get the most time out of their day.

If you are staying overnight on Scilly, load your luggage into the container for your island at Penzance Harbour and attach a colour coded label to your bags. If you're staying on St Mary's you can have it delivered to your accommodation for a small fee (write where you're staying on your luggage label) or pick it up on the quayside when you arrive. Some accommodation providers will pick up you and your luggage by arrangement, otherwise you may need to book a taxi.

If you're staying on an off-island your luggage will be automatically transferred onto your off-island ferry at Hugh Town Quay and will be unloaded at your destination quay. Most accommodation providers will arrange to meet you at the quay to help you with your bags when you arrive. www.islesofscilly-travel.co.uk

BY SKYBUS

Skybus flies to Scilly all year round from Land's End Airport. You can also fly direct to St Mary's Airport from Newquay and Exeter airports; this is a more seasonal service. The flight from Land's End Airport takes about twenty minutes, from Newquay about thirty minutes and from Exeter about sixty minutes. A shuttle bus runs between the train station and Land's End Airport – you will need to book a seat in advance and should aim to leave Penzance Station an hour before your scheduled take-off time. You can also get a taxi from the station. www.islesofscilly-travel.co.uk

BY HELICOPTER FROM PENZANCE

There is a helicopter service from Penzance Heliport (near Sainsbury's as you come into Penzance on the A30) to St Mary's Airport and Tresco. The flight time from Penzance Heliport is about 15 minutes. On-site secure parking is available, as well as a shuttle from the train station. Bookings can be made on their website www.penzancehelicopters.co.uk or by calling T: (01736) 780828.

FERRIES AND SIGHTSEEING BOAT TRIPS

INTER-ISLAND FERRIES

Ferries run between the inhabited off-islands throughout the year. There's a reduced service out-of-season when you may need to book ahead. During the season (roughly end of March/Easter to the end of October) ferries usually start leaving at about 10.15am with returns throughout the day until late afternoon (subject to tide, weather and time of year). Buy your ticket at the kiosk on Hugh Town Quay or on-board. St Mary's Boatman's Association run most of the trips from St Mary's. If you're staying on an off-island, it will have its own boat service that runs daily services to St Mary's plus a rotating mix of circular and evening trips throughout the week. In addition to their main ferry, most have a smaller jet boat used for private charter and water taxi runs. Details of services are on social media and chalked on departure boards around the islands. Tresco, Bryher and St Martin's have more than one quay; your boatman will let you know where the return boat will pick you up.

SIGHTSEEING BOAT TRIPS

All island boat services offer circular sightseeing trips around the uninhabited islands during the season. With the exception of Samson, these don't land but afterwards you can usually land on the nearest inhabited off-island to stretch your legs, get a cup of tea and return on a later boat.

Samson

This is the only uninhabited island where ferries regularly land and it's a highlight of many holidays on Scilly. There are abandoned houses and prehistoric tombs to visit. Remember to take water, sun cream and a picnic with you as there are no cafés, shops or loos. Twin this trip with a visit to Bryher or Tresco.

St Mary's Circular

A circular trip around the whole island. A taste of the open sea and, if the tide permits, coming into some of the bays and inlets like Porth Hellick and Pelistry. A good choice for getting your bearings when you first arrive on Scilly as you'll pass all the other inhabited isles.
Trip takes 1¼ hours.

The Eastern Isles

This is probably the most popular sightseeing trip and the one with the calmest sea conditions. Great for watching and getting close to seabirds and Atlantic grey seals.
Trip takes 1¾ hours, also lands on St Martin's.

Annet, Western Rocks and the Bishop Rock Lighthouse

This boat trip is dependant on sea conditions being calm. If they're not, it might not run for a week or more, so if you have the opportunity, take it. If it's too rough to go all the way to the Bishop Rock Lighthouse, a shorter 1¼ hour trip runs to Annet for seals and seabirds.
Trip takes 2½ hours, also lands on St Agnes.

The Norrard (Northern) Rocks

A trip to the rocks and reefs to the west of Samson and Bryher – Illiswilgig, Scilly Rock and the Garden of the Maiden Bower. Look out for grey seals and puffins.
Trip takes 1½ hours, lands on Bryher/Tresco.

Holy Isles and Round Island Lighthouse

A trip around the small isles between Tresco and St Martin's – Round Island, St Helen's, Teän and Men-a-vaur.
Trip takes 1½ hours, also lands on Tresco, Bryher or St Martin's.

Follow the Gig Races

Follow the gig races from a sightseeing boat. Women race on Wednesday evenings and men on Friday evenings. The courses vary and trips often end up in an off-island pub.

Seabird Specials and Wildlife

Trips throughout the year to different parts of Scilly and the open sea. Includes evening trips to catch the return of shearwaters and puffins to Annet. Puffins are around from April to late July; shearwaters stay a few weeks later.

Ancient Scilly

Hear about the history and archaeology of Scilly with an expert on-board commentary as you cruise the islands.

Evening Supper Trips

A popular trip from St Mary's to the Turk's Head pub on St Agnes but other islands have similar specials too.